Freedom From Financial Shame

Our Non-Highlight Reel

© Traci Vanderbush 2019

Within your hands you hold a simple, personal journey that is crafted to encourage you throughout your own financial journey.

Traci Vanderbush
Celebration, FL
tracivanderbush.wix.com/vanderbush

"Giving thanks is the wealthiest thing you can do."
~Henry Vanderbush

Foreword

I've witnessed it too many times: men and women sitting before us, tear-filled eyes, heads hung low with shame because of their financial situation. I've listened to men tell their stories of working overtime, tiring themselves to misery as they struggle to keep a roof over their children's heads, to keep them fed, to maintain their dental care and medical needs. "I'm working all the hours I possibly can, yet I'm barely able to pay all the bills," one strong man said as his chin quivered. "I'm so embarrassed. How will my kids even go to college?" And yes, these are tithing people who serve God.

I've watched mothers strive to pick up the messes left behind by men who broke their promises. These women balance motherhood and fatherhood, working jobs, keeping house, and hoping to be there for children when they become sick. Employer's demands push them and override their ability to spend precious time with their kids. Shame settles on them like a wet blanket as they question themselves, doubting that they'll ever be able to succeed.

I've witnessed those things, yet I have also known too many miracles to be quiet. Time and time again, the stories of redemption, empowerment, and invading the impossible have been told. Walking in shame and hopelessness is not what we were born for. Your time of difficulty only paints an opening for a glorious masterpiece to be revealed down the road. It's time to lift the financial shame and launch into a new mindset.

The majority of the first twenty-three years of our marriage was spent living on the edge financially. Before sharing a few stories of various jobs and hilarity, I must tell you that we know what it's like to stand in that W.I.C. line, we know what it's like to have to put groceries back on the shelf and remove items at the checkout, and we know what it's like to have a car (make that two) repossessed, and we know what it's like to be sued, and we know what it's like to struggle to keep the electric turned on, even while faithfully tithing and giving offerings with joy. But what I can guarantee you is that we worked very hard the whole time, and God always did something miraculous. Our finances never added up on paper, but God made a way for the impossible, so much so, that people thought we were well-off financially, even when we weren't. Those circumstances ultimately built our faith and trust, enlarging our vision so that we could believe for something greater.

My desire in sharing pieces of our personal journey is to lift financial shame off of those who have been living under condemnation as they strive to live the American Dream. I hope you enjoy the funny stories, the trials, and miracle stories in the following pages. I promise, you will be able to look back at your journey and laugh, too.

Peace to you.

~Traci

[In the following pages, I will share some of our own stories, experiences, and revelations. For more practical tools and deeper insight into Kingdom finances, I highly recommend that you check out **When Heaven Invades Your Finances** by Jim Baker. Jim is a dear friend and pastor of Zion Christian Fellowship in Powell, Ohio. Their church is marked by worship, a strong presence of God, healings, miracles, several dead raisings, and a passion for personal and regional transformation. Jim is the best teacher on finances that I have come across. You can access his resources at: BakersEquip.com, which includes free mp3 downloads of the eighteen-part sermon series, When Heaven Invades Your Finances.]

The American Dream

"If you want your children to turn out well, spend twice as much time with them and half as much money." Abigail Van Buren

The American Dream. It's a well-known concept that we all hope to acquire. Societal expectations loom and we adopt its demands as our commission for life, feeling that if we fall short of the expectations, we are failures. At an early age, we are set up to feel the weight of the dream: "What do you want to be when you grow up? What kind of job are you going to work? Where will you go to college? How are you going to make money?" I remember, as a high school student, bearing the weight of such questions that infused me with panic because all I really wanted to do was raise a family, love people and serve God. How would such things fit into the mold of living "the American Dream?"

Once I married Bill, the next set of questions loomed: "How will you pay for having children? Have you started putting money away for your children's college fund?" *Put money away for college? We're just trying to keep the lights on and keep ourselves fed.* Throughout life, the questions never cease: "Do you have health insurance, life insurance, and retirement set up?" *Breathe. Breathe. Gosh, I barely have enough for gasoline to get me to work each day, but I can't let them know that.*

My husband and I felt called to ministry. I have never met one person who went into ministry to make money. In fact, the majority of people who enter ministry are multi-vocational.

Multiple jobs are required in order to sustain day-to-day living, especially when your family begins growing and you realize that children require more than you could have imagined. Medical, dental, eye care, food, clothing, etc. But one amazing fact stands true to this day; God truly supplied every need. And even when we lacked, somehow it all worked out. It was in those moments of lack that we learned Who our source is, and it also built our faith. We learned how strong we are, and even when the system of the world seemed to crush us, we learned humility and compassion.

All of this to say, the reason I felt compelled to write this little book is to lift the shame of financial struggle off of people. Over the last few years, we have had multiple people come to us with their heads hung low and pain on their face as they express their financial struggles. One good, hard-working, tithing father sat before us, tears streaming down his face. "I work so hard to give my family a good life. I work overtime and still can barely pay our basic bills. How do you guys do it? Why isn't God blessing me?" Ugh. The look in his desperate eyes struck me with an urgency to lift shame off of his heavy heart.

Our response to him was to first let him know he wasn't alone. We shared some of our stories with him and how God brought us through. I loved watching the burden lift from his spirit, and at the end of the conversation he expressed deep gratitude for knowing he wasn't alone. "I had no idea you guys ever had financial hardship." Wow. And that is where most of us who are struggling, or have struggled find ourselves isolated, believing the lie that we are less than, inferior to, and just not as smart/blessed as others who seem to have found the way to financial abundance. The truth is that most everyone has experienced lack and challenges along the way. Even many of the most successful people have known bankruptcy, hunger, and multiple losses along the way to their success.

In the following pages, I want to share some of our story to encourage you and lift guilt and shame from your heart. By the way, at the time of this writing, while we live a good life and have been blessed in many ways, we still do not meet all of the expectations of the great, American dream, and in the eyes of some, we still lack a basic necessity or two. However, we are very content, and in our eyes, we live richly. I have learned that status and labels are really nothing. The amount of money in your bank account, the brands you wear, the assets (or lack of assets) that you have do not carry the power to dictate how you live. With God, it is absolutely true that all things are possible. He is not captive to our world system, and He lives within us.

Bill and Traci at age 5

Oh, How Far We Have Come

Bill was the child of traveling evangelists who lived on very little. He spent most of his growing-up years living in an RV as they went from place to place. His dad, Henry, knew poverty, having lived on a farm in Minnesota during some very rough years: lack of heat in the middle of harsh winters, only a bit of food to share between seven children, etc. Bill's mom grew up as the daughter of a pastor, and she lost her mother at a very young age. Bill's parents knew well the value of a dollar and they thanked God for every bit they had. Compare this to my parents, who were much younger. My mom was only fifteen years old when she became pregnant. Miraculously, she and my dad are still together to this day. They beat the odds. If anyone ever tells you that circumstances surrounding someone's pregnancy and birth have the ability to predict a child's future, just look at me and tell them they are wrong.

At the age of five (1977), I lived with my parents in an old trailer park in Austin, Texas. One day, as Bill's parents were driving their RV through a rainstorm in Austin, a man flagged them down. Wondering why the man was trying to get their attention, Bill's dad pulled over. The man asked if they needed a place to park their RV, and he recommended the North Lamar Trailer Park. Long story short, Bill ended up being my next door neighbor. Two creative five-year-olds, living side-by-side. One particular event, however, began a tight friendship.

My young mother was a hippie who had taken up belly dancing. It was a normal, daily routine for her to practice her sword dance. In my small world, I thought everyone's mother was a belly dancer and that dancing with a sword was a normal activity. One particular day, my mom worked on balancing the sword on her head. With arms spread wide, she began spinning around as the sword remained balanced in place, but her foot accidentally bumped our little television stand, which sent the sword plummeting into her leg. As soon as I saw blood oozing from her leg, I charged out the door and ran to "little Billy's" house. I banged on the door and his mother, Ronda answered. I quickly explained, with my thick, Texas accent, "My momma stabbed herself with a sword!" I remember Ronda's eyes going wide with bewilderment. She called for Bill's dad and they quickly came to my mother's aid. That began a journey of his parents taking my parents under their wing, introducing them to things like "revival." My parents were already believers who regularly attended Baptist church, but this other church culture was a whole new world.

Bill and I played together daily for almost two years. Making mud pies, building forts, playing spy, and watching Looney Tunes together made up our days of childhood innocence. In our minds, we were the richest kids around. We had all the cookies, Jello, and macaroni anyone could ever want, and I thought I was a big deal as I went door-to-door, carrying a 2-liter of Coca Cola, selling cups of Coke for 25 cents. Surprisingly, many neighbors obliged and I was in business. I saw myself as being richer than Bill (I had color TV and he had black and white TV), and my trailer was longer than his. Isn't that hilarious? What I didn't realize is that the nice people who were coming into the trailer park with various Bible lessons and treats actually saw us as children living in poverty, who needed Jesus, and we were their ministry. Honestly, our parents took great care of us. We were clean, well-fed and happy, and exposed to the things of God.

It's actually a miracle that Bill ever married me, because I was the reason for him getting a spanking. As trailer park kids, we were good at creating ways to have fun with little. When we weren't swinging on a water hose that was cleverly hung in a tree, one of our favorite past times was bouncing on old metal fencing once it had become slightly dilapidated. It was a simple procedure of hanging on the top part of the fence until it bent over enough that you could climb on top and bounce away. Bill's dad got tired of looking at the eyesore behind their trailer, so he installed new fencing. He warned Bill, "Now, Billy, that's a brand new fence. You kids don't go bending it down. Do you understand me?" Bill nodded, "Yes."

Within a few days, other neighborhood kids came along, admiring the new fence. Apparently it presented a challenge, so they began hanging and pulling on it until it was bent over enough to become a new toy. Once they had pulled it down, I joined in. Later that day, Bill came over to play with me and I suggested we bounce on it. He stared at me like a deer in the headlights as I jumped onto it and began to bounce. Somewhere in the process, I think he figured that since he hadn't been the one to destroy the fence, it was okay for him to benefit from the destructive power of others, so he hopped aboard and bounced. When his dad came outside to find Bill sitting on the fence, his dad, who was normally very gentle and forever laughing, had a look of confusion on his face. Bill describes his look as "Oh, my gosh…you really want to die?" Hence, the boy received a spanking due to my enticement. But he married me anyway.

For me, the reality of status and different levels of living hit me somewhere in First Grade. I was invited to a classmate's birthday party at his home. Little Robby. What I was not prepared for was the fact that little Robby's house was large, and it even had stairs! *Who has stairs in their house?* That was the first time I recall going home with a feeling of dissatisfaction. Also, that year, I learned a shocking truth when I stood in front of the class for

Show-and-Tell. I was so excited to show my paper ship that came with my kid's meal at Long John Silvers. The paper ship was a big deal to me because my family was too poor to eat out very often. My mom was an expert in making delicious meals out of things like eggs, macaroni and rice. One of my favorite dishes was a fried egg on top of rice. I believed it to be gourmet. When my family had the opportunity to venture out to eat, it was a big deal. I remember that evening at Long John Silvers, staring starry-eyed at the menu. *So many things I can try!* When I learned that I could get fish and hushpuppies inside of a pirate ship, I was ecstatic. I couldn't wait to tell my friends at school.

Finally, the day for Show-and-Tell arrived. When it came my turn, I had the full attention of the classroom as I carefully pulled my cherished boat from a bag. "My family took me to Long John Silvers and I got to eat my fish and hushpuppies from this pirate ship," I happily explained. A few kids began to laugh. The teacher silenced them and I continued, "See, the food was underneath of the sail, but when you lift the pirate's sail, you can eat what's under it." Laughter. One boy hollered, "That's nothing! Everybody eats at Long John Silvers and we all know about this!" I remember staring at the classroom, feeling as if someone punched me in the stomach. My excitement had been punished for being born of ignorance.

I wondered if I really was stupid. *Everyone gets to eat there?* "That's nothing special. It's a paper boat," the boy shouted as kids laughed. As I looked for the teacher's direction, I saw the look of sadness on her face as she tried to shut down the mocking. Things changed for me that day. A little bit of innocence stripped away; not to mention the bit of innocence that a predator neighbor had already taken away. As my school years continued, I learned that my hair had to be a certain way and I needed a certain brand of clothes, and the right kind of shoes in order to be somebody. As expectations grew, my contentment diminished.

A few years later, came a revelatory Christmas. I watched my mom crying, as she slumped into the couch after coming home from work. My dad had also just arrived home from work and he began washing the dishes. "Daddy, why is Mommy crying?" I asked. He sighed, "Well, she's crying because we don't have money to buy Christmas presents." I assured him with a smile, "That's okay! Santa will bring my presents. You don't have to buy anything." He continued scrubbing dishes as I reiterated, "You don't have to buy anything. Santa will bring all the presents." He turned to me, speaking softly, "Santa isn't real." *What!* "Mom and I buy the presents, but we don't have the money this year." That was the day that I recognized the weight that my parents carried.

I wondered if we wouldn't have a place to live. I began to understand the concept of working to make money in order to live, and I also figured out why we were eating at "Mamaw's" house so often. Apparently, it really did take a village to raise children. After that revelation, it became a habit of mine to say to Mamaw, "Thank you for the food and money." Being surrounded by adults who made sure that I had everything I needed and wanted (even those Jordache jeans that I thought I had to have) was the most comforting feeling. There may not have been much money, but with family, we had everything.

Bill and I had small beginnings. Simple, beautiful, small beginnings that some would frown upon. *That's no place to raise a kid.* I heard that one a few times. The culverts in the creek may have been our hideouts and the dirt and gravel on our trailer lots may have been our only yards, but we were content. His dad, Henry, used to say, "Thanksgiving (giving thanks) is the wealthiest thing you can do." He was right. Gratitude maketh rich. That's something that has stuck with me to this day.

Arrested

When Bill and I got married, I was nineteen and he was eighteen years old. I couldn't understand why people scoffed when I showed them my engagement ring. In our eyes, we were fully adult and knew exactly what we were doing. But it was actually the circumstances surrounding the ring that gave us full assurance of our decision, and it was that very thing that built our faith to believe for things we could not afford. At age seventeen, Bill had ventured off to the mountains of Czechoslovakia to build a church with Teen Missions. During his time there, he journaled as he prayed and asked God if he should marry me. "God, I don't have money for an engagement ring, so if I'm supposed to marry Traci, I need a ring." What he did not know was that at the same time, back in the United States, someone approached Bill's parents and gave them a set of wedding bands. The woman said, "These are for your son. He can sell them for money for school, or do what he would like with them." That set of rings fit my finger perfectly!

So knowing we had another force behind our union, I left a full-time job to venture out into something that many regarded as ridiculous: ministry. We had huge goals. Bill laid down his desire to be an actor in Hollywood in order to give his life to bringing the love of Jesus to everyone he met. At the time, he believed he had to choose one or the other. The best plan we could come up with was to go to Bible college (Dallas, Texas) and become youth pastors. We never stopped to consider that such a job wouldn't pay a living wage. We were honestly just living by faith, following the call we felt in our hearts.

We moved into our little campus apartment in the middle of bad territory. The nights we slept on the floor instead of the bed because of gunfire…we kept those details hidden from our parents. *Why worry them?* We lived happily on Ramen noodles, macaroni, and ground beef, not to mention the dollar menu at McDonald's and, hey…two tacos for a dollar at Jack-in-the-Box. We didn't know much about nutrition. We just knew how to eat for little money. Bill worked at the local zoo before moving on to be a house painter. I babysit the children of our professors. Bill did the painting gig until he was momentarily arrested by the police when they mistook him for a burglar while he was scraping paint from a back window in a prominent neighborhood. I think being handcuffed and held to the ground by a cop caused Bill's desire for house painting to diminish, to say the least. However, he was quite excited to call me and tell me, "Hey! I got arrested today!" An experience he would not forget.

An internship for a youth pastorate opened up in a town about half an hour away, so Bill and I happily stepped into a fun-filled chapter of leading young people, doing outreaches, and lock-ins. When the church decided to pay us $75 per week (1992), we were ecstatic! To get paid to do something you are passionate about is wonderful. I remember a particular lock-in (a youth overnight event) that exhausted us terribly. Bill and I were trying to get home but both of us were too tired to drive. We kept pulling over on the side of the road to catch a few minutes of sleep. We noticed we were about to run out of gas, but we had no money. We dug around the car, pulling up the floor mats and plunged our hands into every crevice of the seats until we found 43 cents in change. We paid the cashier at the gas station and asked him to set the pump to stop at 43 cents. Thankfully, that was enough to get us home where we slept before heading to school the next morning.

While carrying our son in utero during one particular July in the Texas heat, Bill and I prepared to drive to one of our jobs on the other side of the city. A 35-minute drive without air conditioning in the car was especially uncomfortable and potentially dangerous while pregnant, so we had the brilliant idea of filling a metal bowl with ice and placed it between us in the car. We directed the A/C vents onto the ice, thinking that perhaps it would create a bit of cool air, but instead, I ended up with ice water spilled in my lap as Bill turned a corner. At least it was cold. We continued on to the job and cleaned the man's house, doing all of his laundry for fifty dollars. We were thankful for every bit of money we could acquire.

Gratitude filled our hearts in everything we did. I quite believe we were too naive to realize that the way we lived would be appalling to people, but we were happy together. Everything was an adventure. We graduated from Bible college, and I remember the delight of walking across the stage in my cap and gown, pregnant belly and all. Our next chapter took us to Austin, Texas where we worked as children's and youth pastors. We learned a lot of valuable lessons (there is a book that I would rewrite if I had time that's floating around on the internet called Walking With A Shepherd, which covers that season). We had two children during our days as youth pastors. With each child, we were growing a bit more concerned about having enough money to support a family. My husband willingly worked multiple jobs so that I could stay home and raise our children. Now, that's an amazing man!

Living on Little

"Simplicity is the ultimate sophistication."
Leonardo da Vinci

The majority of the first twenty-three years of our marriage was spent living on the edge financially. Before sharing a few stories of various jobs and hilarity, I must tell you that we know what it's like to stand in that W.I.C. line, we know what it's like to have to put groceries back on the shelf or even at the checkout, and we know what it's like to have a car (make that two) repossessed, and we know what it's like to be sued, and we know what it's like to struggle to keep the electric turned on. But what I can guarantee you is that we worked very hard the whole time, and God always did something miraculous. And in case you're wondering, yes, we regularly paid tithes. Our finances never added up on paper, but God made a way for the impossible, so much so, that people thought we were well-off financially, even when we weren't.

Before I continue with a few stories, here are a few of the jobs that Bill worked while pastoring:

Children's Pastor
Youth Pastor (24/7)
Senior Pastor (24/7)
Blockbuster Video Sales
House Painter
Zoo Membership Salesman
Credit Card Salesman
House Cleaner

Limousine Driver/Chauffeur
Bookstore Manager
Animation Studio Manager
Receptionist for Psychotherapy Office
Pizza Maker
Pizza Delivery Driver
A&R Rep for Grapetree Records (Rap Label)
Underwater Videographer
Shelving Installer
Wedding Videographer
Crepe Maker/Cook
Business owner
…and MANY more

Intertwined in that list would be the jobs that I worked in frame-making and glass cutting while Bill was a Senior Pastor. I also had the privilege of working with a Foster Care and Adoption agency in which I got to help create families. But there are some funny stories in the mix, as well as some crazy risk-taking moments in our work history. One of my favorite stories was during our venture into cleaning the home of actress Sandra Bullock during construction.

House Cleaning Blunder

Through a series of hilarious happenstance, Bill was given the job of supervising the cleaning crew during the construction of a home that actress Sandra Bullock was building. I remember his first day on the job well. I was at home, schooling our children, when the phone rang. It was already after noon and Bill was huffing and puffing, "What is a *du vet* cover?" he asked. I responded, "Do you mean a duvet (doo-vey) cover?" He paused for a moment, "Yeah, whatever it's called." I gave him a quick lesson in the correct pronunciation and informed him that duvet covers envelop comforters. Silence. I asked, "What did you do?" Bill proceeded to explain that he thought duvet covers were a rich person's fancy mattress cover and that he had put the mattresses inside of the duvet covers. Not one, not two, not three. He did all eight beds before deciding to call me. "I really need your help, Traci." That began a few months of us both working in Ms. Bullock's home.

Bill's most memorable time on that job was the day he was going through the house, watering plants. He held his watering can prim and proper-like, as he nurtured each plant along the hallway. Ms. Bullock came down the hallway, so Bill quickly turned aside to tend to a plant in order to avoid talking with her (this was standard policy for workers). As he poured water onto the plant, she stopped and said, "You do know that's a fake plant, right?" Bill was horrified as he grasped for words. She asked, "You don't do this for a living, do you?" He explained that he was actually a pastor of a church and they had a good laugh together.

Billy V And His Rap Days

Shortly after Bill became a Senior Pastor (something he said he would never do) at the age of twenty-five, he found himself invited to work for a rap label called Grapetree Records. Bill was an Artist & Repertoire representative. He enjoyed picking up artists from the airport, meeting about record deals, taking part in creating music videos and working with people like Prime Minister, E-Roc, Antonious, Amani, Ayeesha, Bruthaz Grimm, Lil' Raskull, and many other names. It was during his time of employment there that we finally knew what it was like to have health insurance and enough money to buy a decent car.

I recall the day we drove to church in that used Oldsmobile Aurora. One of the church leaders commented, "Wow! Look who's rolling in the dough." Those words returned to my memory the time when we were youth pastors. We drove an old minivan with two rotting tires. When metal finally made itself visible through the rubber, we opened a credit line with the local tire shop so we could get the four cheapest tires available. Those same words were spoken when we showed up at church in the old van with brand new tires: "Wow! Look who's rolling in the dough. All new tires." Ugh. I admit that I felt rage rise up within me in that moment. *People have no idea how hard my husband works behind the scenes, and it'll be a struggle to pay off these tires!*

It dawned on me that day in the Oldsmobile Aurora, that you just couldn't win with church people when it came to personal finances and their judgments. As long as we were in ministry, we would be analyzed and our finances would never private. Our bank account would always be under scrutiny, and our every move would be judged. There were often arguments amongst leaders and congregants as to whether or not the staff were being paid too much or too little. Some felt that the pastoral staff should be paid more so they'd be available for the many needs of the church and meet those needs without distraction.

Others felt that pastors should not be paid anything, and should have to work 'regular jobs like everyone else.' Yet those same people would become angry if the pastors worked other jobs and were not available when a need arose. I quickly learned that it didn't matter how little or how much a pastor had, how available or unavailable he/she was…there would always be judgment about our perceived financial situation and we would always be under a microscope. We enjoyed nice paychecks from Bill's job as A&R Rep with the rap label, but we soon felt the tug to be fully available to the church, so Bill slipped back into "full-time" ministry, and we took a pay cut.

A Pastor With Soggy Pizza

Months later, as a full-time pastor, we didn't want anyone to know that Bill was working five jobs at one time. I fulfilled office duties, scheduled our monthly elders, deacons, and ministry leader's meetings, answered phones, typed documents, orchestrated nursery schedules, and taught Sunday School, all while educating my children. I enjoyed planning our annual mission's banquets, however, people were not happy with me when I decided one year, that our meal would be rice and beans. I wanted everyone to identify with the hungry. Yeah…that didn't go over so well. One particular congregant complained to me, "I purposefully didn't eat a lot today because I was looking forward to the banquet. Are you serious that all we're getting is rice and beans?" *Well, the banquet is supposed to evoke interest in raising funds for the hungry, so…* (insert laughing face here).

During that season, Bill went straight from the church office into making and delivering pizzas. He remembers a particular evening when one of our deacons came into the pizza restaurant to put in an order. The man stood at the counter waiting for his pizza, not noticing the entire time, that his pastor was the one making it. Bill thought it was hilarious. He threw on the toppings and put the pizza into the oven, disguised by the apron and hat, evading eye contact. The order was fulfilled and the deacon left without a clue that his pastor had made his pizza. Bill then loaded the car with deliveries and set out to take the orders to their destination. A massive thunderstorm rolled in as he drove from place to place. Soaking wet, he made his final delivery, and the last two people did not tip him.

Bill returned home; I heard the car pull up in the driveway. After a couple of minutes, I wondered why it was taking him so long to come inside. I opened the front door to check on him, and there he sat on the front step, soggy and head hung low. I asked, "What's wrong?" He shook his head and muttered, "I got caught in the storm and didn't even get tipped." As he came inside, he chuckled. We remembered his dad's words about giving thanks. Gratitude is power. We pressed through, determined to stay positive. My appreciation for him went through the roof!

I wanted more than anything for my husband to succeed, to be blessed and have it easier. Though he wanted to empower me to be a full-time mom, I took a part-time job in glass and matte cutting, framing and setting poetry. During the hours I spent at that job, Bill took over the curriculum for our children and guided them through their schooling. As soon as I got home, he was off to meet the needs of the church. There is nothing more amazing to me than men who want to care of their families, and Bill certainly paid a price to take care of his. Soggy pizza and all.

A Supernatural Event That Changed Everything

"It is abnormal for a Christian not to have an appetite for the impossible. It has been written into our spiritual DNA to hunger for the impossibilities around us to bow at the name of Jesus."
Bill Johnson

There are numerous other stories I could mention as Bill worked various jobs, but more importantly, there were some supernatural events that took place that began to shift things for us. It seemed that in the middle of jobs and keeping ministries running, being on-call 24/7, visiting families at 3am during issues of domestic violence, making hospital and jail visits, and all of the things that go along with pastoral leadership, we began to experience some miracles along the way.

One of the first miracles that I remember was when our son, Britain, was extremely ill with a very high fever at the age of two. I had taken him to the doctor earlier in the day, where I was told to keep an eye on him and watch for signs of lethargy. That night, Britain's fever was escalating and he laid on the floor, not wanting to move. As I was about to call the doctor, Bill and I laid hands on him and began praying out loud. Within a few seconds, Britain suddenly sat straight up, staring at the wall behind us. We both turned to see what he was looking at. Britain pointed and said, "He's big." We looked, but could not see what our son saw.

Instantly, Britain got up and started running around and playing with toys. His fever was totally gone!

When our daughter, Sara, was four years old, she was in the bathroom singing loudly: "Praise Adonai." She had picked up those words from a worship song. I listened as she sang for a good three minutes and then she called out, "Mommy! Mommy! Come and look!" I walked into the bathroom and she was looking up in awe. I asked her what she saw. "Look, Mommy! Can you see the rain? It was raining in here. It was like bubbles and they all came down the walls and everywhere!" Her excited smile lit her eyes with a joy that was tangible. I couldn't see what she saw, but I could feel the presence of God.

Over the years, our children began having very vivid, prophetic dreams, and they often had amazing words of wisdom for us that were far beyond their years. Both of them could see things that we could not, and we realized that some very real visits from another realm were occurring. Bill and I were hungry for more and we gradually grew weary of church politics and religious organizations and competition that we witnessed amongst believers. We knew there was so much more to this thing called Christianity and we wanted to see the Kingdom clearly.

In 2005, Bill called a few of the leadership together to pray on a Saturday morning. Our worship leader, a couple of deacons, and our children were there in the sanctuary as we prayed. Bill found himself saying, "Let the rain of Your presence fall on us, God." We didn't know what we were asking for. It just sounded like a nice, poetic way to pray. A couple of minutes later, we noticed that water was dripping from the ceiling. A little drip here and a little drip there...but within seconds, it quickly multiplied until the entire ceiling of our large sanctuary was dripping like crazy! It had started in one small area, and we watched as the moisture quickly spread. Several of us ran, looking for rolls of plastic in the storage room. We covered the musical instruments, the sound board, and as many chairs as we possibly could. The building and everything in it was brand new. The only water source in the ceiling was the fire sprinkler system, but water was falling in areas that were not near the sprinkler lines.

Bill ran outside to the truck to get his phone, ready to chew out the building contractor and demand that he get there quickly to fix the problem. *This is a new building! How could this happen?* Our son, who was ten years old at the time, ran outside after his dad. Britain did his typical happy jig in the parking lot as he hollered, "Dad, look! It's not raining outside, but it's raining in the sanctuary!" Bill looked up and realized there was not a cloud in the sky. It was a bright, blue day and there hadn't been rain in days. Bill recalls that in that moment, he felt God speak to him strongly: "If I pour out what You are asking for, the same reaction you just had will be the reaction of your people. 'This is bad, this is wrong, and this is going to ruin everything!'" Bill was stunned. He asked God to forgive him for not recognizing what He was doing, and he repented for his attitude.

When Bill walked back into the sanctuary, I was in the process of noticing that there was no more moisture. The ceiling was completely dried up and where rain had fallen on the plastic, only dust remained. The chairs, the carpet, the instruments were dry. No moisture whatsoever. The building was dried up within fifteen minutes. We wrapped up the plastic and left in awe, slightly speechless. Bill remembered that God said the people would react negatively, so he said, "Don't tell anyone about this." But the very next day (Sunday), Bill couldn't help himself. He shared the story with the congregation. A couple of people seemed excited, but as soon as church was over, we had people coming up to us with explanations: "If the humidity level is just right and the temperature outside, blah, blah, blah…" The 'ifs' and potential explanations were like dung to us because we had seen a literal, nonstop rainfall that spread from tiny to large, and then was gone, leaving no trace of its presence. We knew it was a supernatural event, and we didn't want to miss out on the invitation that God was placing before us.

We hung on and continued ministering at that church for a bit, but the fire that was burning inside of us left us with a knowing that a new chapter was about to open. During this time, Bill was not only Senior Pastor, but he also traveled weekly for a company called Career Track. A typical week was me holding down the fort, the needs of the congregation, and teaching our children at home while Bill flew out three weeks per month to teach businesses how to deal with difficult people. Literally, one of the courses he taught was called "Dealing With Difficult People." I would pick him up from the airport on Friday evenings, we'd spend Saturday together as a family, he would preach on Sundays and then I'd drive him back to the airport on Sunday nights. We did that routine for one year, somehow, by the grace of God. But that job made it possible to stay on top of the bills and live in a modest home of our own.

One morning while Bill was out of town for work, I had a sudden knowing...it was time to resign the church. It was clear as day. The phone rang and I answered. Bill was on the other end of the line. His first question to me was, "Are you hearing anything from God?" The way he asked the question was clue that he knew something. I replied, "Yes. It's time to go." He responded excitedly, "Yes! That's what I heard, too!" We had not planned to leave the church, but the fact that we both had that same specific word on the same morning was all we needed to step out and take a risk. We had no plan B. All we knew is that it was time to go. We resigned the church, not having any idea how we would maintain our mortgage once he resigned, so we put our home on the market. The realtor informed us that houses in our area were sitting on the market for an average of eighty-four days, so she wanted us to be prepared. We got an offer within twenty-four hours! We made a few phone calls, and thanks to my mom who called a family friend, we had a small guest house to rent on their property. We accepted the offer on our house and moved to the other side of the city two weeks later.

The little two-bedroom, limestone guest house in the woods was the perfect retreat for our weary souls. The last couple of years of ministry had left us a bit jaded, wounded, and ready for something different. Our wonderful friends, Michael and Meri Reed, were the best landlords, greeting us with a smile every morning. Their home was right across the driveway from the guest house and they charged us a small amount of rent when they could have charged more. Bill and I didn't go to church for quite awhile. After twelve solid years of nonstop ministry, we were in no hurry to be part of a church, yet Michael and Meri invited us into their house church, and it was a most life-giving season. Ever patient, ever loving, ever giving, and always encouraging, they nourished our hearts and souls back to life.

One day, Michael informed us that a man named Bill Johnson would be speaking in town. "You guys really should go," he encouraged. The last thing that Bill and I wanted to do was go to church or a conference, however, I had started listening to a CD of one of Bill Johnson's messages and it flowed with the love of Jesus in a way that I hadn't heard in a long time. I tried to get my Bill to listen to the CD. I'd turn it on and he would turn it off. Finally, one night, Bill fell into a deep sleep. He woke himself up saying these words, **"What you know will keep you from what you need to know, if you don't remain a novice."** He sat up in bed, wondering what in the world he was muttering to himself. He took note and wrote the words down on a piece of paper next to the bed.

The next night, we attended the Bill Johnson conference (my husband went reluctantly). The church was packed out by the time we got there, so we stood in the back against the wall. Worship was incredible, and when Bill Johnson got up to speak, all he talked about was Jesus. The first statement he made that really grabbed our attention was, "Jesus is the most normal Christian in the

Bible." We pondered that as he stood in silence for a moment. Then he said, "Jesus Christ **is** perfect theology." *Oh my gosh! How did I never see this? We spent time in apologetics and Biblical debates for years, trying to hammer out what Christianity means, and we had ridiculous theological debates! You mean it's as simple as Jesus? Of course! Jesus said, "If you've seen Me, you've seen the Father."* These simple statements carried so much weight and were powerful enough to remove the blinders. Then Bill Johnson looked straight at the back of the room, right where Bill and I were standing. He said, "What you know will keep you from what you need to know, if you don't remain a novice." I looked at my husband as his mouth dropped open. We were stunned. That night was the first time we felt like new believers who were overwhelmed with the good news of the Gospel. This began a healing and faith-building journey for us, yet we still had some massive mountains to overcome along the way.

A Hawaiian Dream

"Aloha ke Akua."
God is love.

While living at the Reed's guest home, Bill took a job at a computer software company. We were content to live like "normal" people and have a normal life, hidden away in the woods and without the demands of ministry life. We had no idea that a wild new chapter in Hawaii awaited us. When Bill and I were dating, we used to throw these words into the air, "Wouldn't that be cool to live in Hawaii someday?" I don't know that we ever believed it would happen. We just thought it was a nice idea and I knew that my grandmother always had a great love for Hawaii.

For fun, Bill looked online to see if there were any job openings there, and he happened across an ad for an underwater videographer. "I've always wanted to dive for a living! And I love to film," he exclaimed. I suggested he check it out, so he did. It was on the island of Maui, and Bill remembered that his dad used to preach for a man in Maui named Robb Finberg. Bill contacted him, and long story short, we ended up moving to Maui for one year where Bill worked on staff with Robb, and he did underwater videography at Molokini Crater three times per week.

It was a dream of a year. Work was good. The island was amazing. We lived on the side of Haleakala volcano which gave us panoramic views of the island valley, the ocean, and two other islands. That year, we witnessed numerous miracles as we launched what we called the Maui School of Supernatural Ministry. When we announced the first meeting, we thought perhaps 30 people would show up, but on the first night, 200 people showed up! There are many stories I could tell about healing, salvation, restoration, resurrection from death, and more, but that would be another book (to read just a few, visit journalofmiracles.blogspot.com/2007/). That season ended with one of Hawaii's sacred men, standing atop the volcano at his altar, and dedicating the island to Jesus.

During that year, I had taught my children a lot about how we live under the protective "wings" of God. "He will cover you with His feathers." We talked about angels. We talked about angels and a funny thing happened: feathers started showing up overnight in our home, just outside of the kid's bedrooms. Each morning, there would be a pile of white feathers. At first, we thought that birds were getting into the house, but we finally realized that wasn't the case. One day as we drove down Haleakala volcano, Bill and I started talking about how wild it was that all those feathers kept showing up. As we were talking about it, a white feather came into the car and fluttered around our heads. "What!?" We started laughing. The kids witnessed it as well, and we all thought it was pretty awesome. The feather suddenly flew out the other window. *What are the chances of that?*

The next day, Bill went to work at Molokini Crater where he would be diving 90-feet deep with sharks. I prayed for him to be safe, asking God to send angels to keep watch over him. Bill arrived home that day so excited. "You've got to see this!" He pulled out the video camera. "Look what I caught on film at 90-feet down." I watched as fish swam by, and then, there it was. A big white feather floated right up to the camera. It seemed that everyday in Maui was a miracle, but I was feeling the tug of family in Texas, and Bill's dad's health began to decline. At the one year mark, we made the decision to move back to Texas, and that move first plummeted us into an exciting year of ministry, and then everything went dark.

The American Dream. We were getting somewhat close to seeing that reality. Things held fairly steady and we decided to buy a house. We chose a lot, a floor plan, and we carefully picked flooring, doors, cabinets, and fixtures. Daily, we walked that lot before the foundation was ever poured. We prayed over the land, and when the structure was going up, we wrote scripture verses in every room, anointed the concrete and doorframes. It was a dream come true! However, one week prior to closing on the house, we had to back out due to a life change that was ignited by Bill's anger toward God for the failing health of his father. We found ourselves flailing as we tried to make the right decisions for our family. The house was gone. The job was gone. There was no plan. Everything just came to a grinding halt.

We put our belongings into storage and packed our bags. We drove to Minnesota for the summer and lived in Bill's parent's home in a tiny town of 300 people. The quiet was good for us, and the acres of farmland provided peaceful scenery that breathed, "Slow down. Listen. Just be." But you could only "just be" for so long. We needed income and we needed a plan. During our time there, Bill briefly worked in a butcher shop and actually had to be part of butchering pigs. I'm pretty sure I made him throw away a couple of blood-spattered shirts. I wasn't good at dealing with that, and neither was he.

It seems that season was a blur and I can't even remember how we ended up without a car. I suppose some unpleasant memories get erased. When it was time to return to Texas to begin a new adventure, we had $1000 to our name. Bill found a van for sale for $900 on Craigslist, so we checked it out. Cash paid. Done deal. We got into the 19-year-old GMC Safari van which wreaked of cat pee. *Great. This is just wonderful.* Our kids were troopers, however. They thought it was great that we had a van. Once we got to the house, we targeted the cat pee smell on the center section of seats and tried every chemical known to remove the odor, but the odor refused to leave. We removed the center section of seats and threw a rug on the floor. The kids thought that was the greatest thing ever. "It's like a limousine back here!" We drove our "limo" to the junkyard and scavenged the grounds for every missing part and piece until the van was better than before. That beloved van became known as "George." Old, faithful George took us from Minnesota to Texas, from Texas to Florida, and then back to Texas…and then to Florida where we sold him for $900. Somehow that old van spoke volumes to me about God's grace and sustaining power. You will notice that throughout hard times, there will be something unusual, or perhaps just simple, that will speak to you on a deep level. Keep an eye out for that during difficult seasons.

The Mind Shift

"Don't spend time beating on a wall, hoping to transform it into a door." Coco Chanel

Somewhere in the valley, there was a particular night when hopelessness weighed on me. As hard as I tried to be a great wife, mom, and minister, I found myself with a heavy heart, perspective skewed, and my thoughts were jaded. We happened to be in Houston for a conference where I sat on the front row, unable to enter the joy of the event. The music played, people danced, but I felt darkness attempting to suffocate me. My mind wondered what was actually true. I didn't trust people. One of my closest friends had wounded me deeply, causing a mind shift.

I found wealth in having great family and friends, but when disappointments came, I had to believe that God was the only one I could dream with, no matter how small or how big. Surely He was the only one I could completely, utterly trust, but even so, my soul wasn't 100% positive. I lay on the floor of the sanctuary, partially under a chair. While people around me cried with joy, I cried tears of sorrow. I hoped they would mistake my tears for the Lord doing a good work in me; and not recognize the tears for what they were…cries of desperation, questioning, and doubting. Before worship ended, I peeled myself off the floor and exited the sanctuary before anyone could try to hug me or engage me in conversation. I just needed to be alone. Alone with God.

I headed across the road and walked until I came to a series of office buildings. In the center was a peaceful fountain surrounded by weeping willows. My heart was drawn to a bench beneath one of the trees. I needed to cry with those trees. I ran my hands along the smooth wooden seat, deciding to recline on it. As I turned onto my side, my eyes rested on the water that flowed toward me before cascading down the sides. *He leads me beside still waters.* Those words rang deep within me. *He leads me beside still waters.* I gazed at the fountain, noticing the stillness of the waters that rested along the edge once they had plummeted to their destination. *Maybe I'm like the waters.* I allowed peace to wash over me.

I looked at the grass around the fountain. *He makes me to lie down in green pastures.* I needed to feel the grass; touch it and experience it as a resting place, but I wasn't willing to leave the comfort of the bench. While the surface was hard, it was a comfort because it was holding me. I pondered how amazing it was that a living thing that God created had become useful in its death, and now brought me comfort. *Could I possibly leave something behind that will bring comfort to someone after I'm long gone? Could this death of ego, death of certain dreams become a comfort to someone else in their own time of questioning?*

He restores my soul. The words of Psalm 23 seemed to vibrate through my entire being. It was a psalm that I had memorized as a child. I won an award in school for reciting it from memory, yet I failed to understand the power of the words that I spoke. But now those words were deeply meaningful. *I think I get it.* The wind blew over me, the weeping willows swayed, I breathed in the comfort of my Father and spoke those words of long ago:

<blockquote>
The Lord is my Shepherd. I shall not want.
In Him, I lack absolutely nothing. There is no need of anything.
He makes me to lie down in green pastures.
He wants me to rest. I have all I need.
He leads me beside still waters.
</blockquote>

The raging waters that I thought would drown me are no longer raging. With God, I am at peace.
He restores my soul.
He loves my soul enough to revive it.
He leads me in the paths of righteousness for His name's sake.
He is true to His word. He sets everything right.
Though I walk through the valley of the shadow of death
Death is only a shadow
I will fear no evil, for You are with me. Your rod and staff comfort me.
There is no reason to fear. His rod of power in my life, and His staff that guides me are for my good, not for my harm.
You prepare a table before me in the presence of my enemies
Those who hurt me will see the Father pouring out His best and finest to me. He prepares a feast for His children. I can forgive them and invite them in to dine with me, so they will know that they were created to be my brothers and sisters.
He anoints my head with oil and my cup runs over.
He nourishes me with everything I need to live out my destiny, despite circumstances.
Surely goodness and mercy will follow me all the days of my life
I cannot escape His goodness and mercy. They follow me, cleaning up the debris and making everything beautiful.
And I will dwell in the house of the Lord forever.
I will always be Home, wherever I am. Everything in my Father's house is mine. I have complete access, and there will never be a day when I do not have access to Him, His heart, and His ways

That night at the fountain began a mind shift for me. There would always be enough. Whether in relationship, life challenges, finances...whatever it may be, there will always be enough. Either I believed it or I did not.

Flipside Crepes

"I'm getting out of the ministry so I can actually make money."
Bill Vanderbush

There are many details that I'm leaving out of this journey of our lives, but there came a time when Bill said, "I'm getting out of ministry so I can actually make money." That led to an opportunity that we were given to run two kiosks in the Amway arena in Orlando, Florida. Bill always enjoyed making crepes for our family on Saturdays. He had been inspired by the crepe makers of Paris years prior when a dear family paid our way to a missions trip in Albania. We had the opportunity to spend two days in Paris on the way to Albania. Watching the artistry of making crepes gave Bill the idea of running his own creperie. When he was presented with having two kiosks in the Amway arena, we jumped at the idea, packed up our things and headed to Florida.

Upon our arrival, we took the little money we had to buy the equipment we would need. After the purchases were made, the NBA went on strike, which totally shut down our opportunity and the man who offered us the kiosks passed away suddenly. There we sat in our new apartment with no income. Bill's fast action to correct the course meant registering with the state as Flipside Crepes, buying a tent and more equipment to travel from event to event. Each weekend, we rented a Uhaul trailer and loaded up our tent and tools. We stayed in cheap hotels where we made our magical crepe batter. We had a few successful events, but we often ended up rained out or at an event that was a bust. Our final event ended with a heavy downpour that left us loading everything up in the mud. Our children were loading items into the van while Bill and I tore down the tent. Upon letting one of the ties loose, a waterfall cascaded onto our heads. We stood drenched and began laughing…because laughter was better than crying.

The next day, we took a stroll through an old tourist section called Old Town. *FOR LEASE.* A sign stood out to us as we passed a small, empty retail space. Bill excitedly announced, "That's it! We have to get that space." I was unsure. Honestly, we didn't have enough money for the space, and we definitely didn't have the credit score they would want. Our credit had taken a hit. But we were out of options, so why not ask? To our great surprise, we ended up getting the space (they must have been desperate to lease it out). We spent a year struggling to maintain a business, our apartment rent, and raising a family. Bill and I found ourselves working 7 days per week, 12-15 hours per day, and we were required to be open 365 days per year. We had signed away our lives.

Even though customers loved our food, it turned out that through multiple marketing ventures and business changes, we were just barely getting by. Every business owner at our location complained of the area being like a ghost town during the weekdays. Into the third month of business, having not had one day off, Bill and I were utterly fried. We finally hired a few employees to help lighten the load. With adding payroll taxes and expenses into the mix, we struggled to have much profit. On one particular afternoon Bill announced to me, "Hey, we made a $300 profit so far today!" The day was beginning to look up. I took a break to drive home to let our dog out for a walk. I first went to the mailbox to check the mail, only to find a tax bill that said we owed another $300. *Well, there went the profit.* I stuffed the bill back into the envelope as I approached the front door. As I started to insert the key into the lock, there it was. A big, red notice on the door informed me that due to being five days behind on rent, we had three days to vacate. Despite the fact that we notified management that we needed an extra week to pay, policies and procedures were being enforced. I unlocked the door to the apartment and fell to my knees on the carpet. Our dog, Sasha, ran to greet me as I cried, "Why, Lord? Why is this so hard? Why? We are working so hard! What more can we do?"

In that moment, I felt His voice vibrate through me with a simple question: **"Do you trust Me?"** Instantly, all fear left. I wiped tears away and stood up with assurance that God knew how hard we were working, and He would make a way where it seemed there was no way out. To this day, those words often serve to remind me that nothing is impossible, and that my job is to dream big. **"Do you trust Me?"** His question has lifted me up during various challenges, and now I see that those challenges are exciting opportunities to watch impossibilities become reality.

The next day, Bill and I dressed up in business attire to make a visit to the apartment complex management office. We handed them $30 and explained the situation we were in. We promised them that each day we would bring money into the office until we were caught up. Thankfully, they were extremely kind. Some days, we were able to pay $15, $50, and other days, $500, until we were back on track. The manager even began sending people to our business to eat. That's called *turning a potential enemy into your advocate.* Thank God.

Each day began with Bill heading to the market at 7:00am to purchase fresh ingredients. We reluctantly removed certain menu items from the menu on days that we weren't able to afford all of the ingredients. Bill had the brilliant idea of highlighting the affordable options as "specials" and he definitely made it extra special. Creativity came into play. Bill also made it a habit to visit the business owners around us to check in on them, seeing what their needs were. We found that we were not alone. It seemed everybody was struggling; even the businesses that had been going for over thirty years. We all became buddies and lifted each other up, sending customers to each other. Some of these business owners were quite anti-Christian, but once they found out we were ministers, they seemed delighted and they often came to us for prayer and direction. This is not something we tried to make happen. Honestly, we were too exhausted to have an agenda! We were just being us. No agenda whatsoever.

I quickly learned to value the camaraderie of people unlike myself. After many years of ministry, we had become accustomed to connecting with fellow believers, but there was such beauty in finding connection with people who would never darken the door of a church. What a priceless year of revelation.

Vampires

*"...but with humility of mind, regard one another
as more important than yourselves."*
The Apostle Paul
Philippians 2:3

Down the road from our business was a haunted house in which a group of vampires were employed. They weren't just pretending to be vampires. They actually took on the persona and practiced a lifestyle of drinking blood. Three of the young men had fangs permanently implanted in their mouths and they wore red contact lenses every day. Black capes flowed behind them as they walked into our restaurant. As I stood at the cash register, I asked one young man, "What can I get for you today?" He leaned over the cash register, red eyes glaring at me, as if to intimidate. In his hand he held a wine goblet filled with red liquid, and he made sure that I saw it. I smiled at him. He opened his mouth to reveal his fangs. I continued smiling, "What can we make for you today?" Finally, he ordered some food. One thing I forgot to mention is that Bill and I prayed over our batter each day, declaring that whoever ate it would be filled with the Holy Spirit. That may sound laughable, but it actually happened multiple times, so I was quite excited to serve a vampire.

The vampire boys began to frequent our place and finally the day came when one of them said to us, "I feel peace here. Would you mind if I just come and sit?" We were delighted. "Of course you can sit here any time." One of them in particular would come sit at our counter every day. He began to open up, pouring his heart out to us, even when we hadn't asked him any questions. He shared that he had grown up in a Christian home, yet he'd been abused and suffered much loss within his family. Our hearts were filled with compassion for him. Bill shared loving words and fatherly grace, and it wasn't long before the young man removed his red contact lenses and stopped wearing his black eye makeup. It seemed the Holy Spirit was doing something in him, and it was time for him to come home. This was just one of many transformations that took place with our customers.

On Father's Day that year, one young man who used to approach us like an enemy, came in. With tear-filled eyes, he gave Bill a handmade bracelet that he had spent several hours making. "Bill, you're the closest thing I have to a father. I wanted you to have this. Thank you for being so kind to me." Bill hugged him, blown away by the young man's change of heart. We saw two more miraculous things that week as well: the drug-dealing business owner across the road from us, who cursed preachers and wanted nothing to do with Bill ended up hugging him, and I had the opportunity to pray for a young man who had cancer...two weeks later, he came in excited beyond words. "My cancer is gone! The doctor can't find any!"

Despite the hardship, exhaustion, and financial devastation, our family experienced beauty in the midst of it all. We could now laugh at the obstacles, knowing that God was very much involved with us in our flailing business venture. We began to feel a shift coming as several friends would randomly call and say, "When are you getting back into ministry? It's time." We honestly didn't know what that would look like, and we didn't know that we were even ready for that. *Besides, who would want to hear anything we had to say?* One morning, we entered our little storefront, switched on the crepe makers, readied the cash register and began organizing ingredients for the day. Shortly after we opened the door, a couple who we've known for several years walked in. They had come from Texas to Florida for a vacation. We were delighted to see them because it had been a long time since we'd talked. It wasn't but a couple of minutes into the conversation that our friend, Lyn, said, "I have something to tell you but I don't know if you'll like it." We were curious and cautious. *Uh oh.* She continued, "I was praying and I clearly felt the Lord saying that your business is coming to a close." Bill and I got excited. *Relief at last!* She spoke confidently, "God is putting something before you and you need to pay attention to it, because it's Him. It's time for you to be back in pastoral ministry."

The idea of the business coming to a close was actually a welcomed, joyful thought because we were tired of the daily struggle. We needed a break. In fact, Bill had told me just the week before, "I feel like I need to be rescued." We thanked our friends for coming to visit and we promised we would consider her words. There was no way they could have known about our situation. For all they knew, we were thriving and rolling in the dough. Now, we had some sense of direction from a friend who didn't know what was happening in our lives.

Exactly one hour later, the phone rang. On the other end of the line was a friend of ours, Bill Hart, a pastor from Texas. He told Bill that he was starting a school of ministry in Austin, and then he said, "I know you're busy running a business in Florida, but I felt like the Lord wanted me to ask you to come and help us launch the school. Would you pray about it?" Wow! Seriously, the morning was starting out in an interesting way. Bill promised to pray about it. He hung up the phone and looked at me, shaking his head in wonder. "What is going on?" We discussed how in the world it would possibly work out. How would we go about closing the business and leave on a good note with the shopping center management? Our apartment lease was coming up in just three weeks and it would be time to renew or move. How would we even afford to move and where would we live? The questions were answered one at a time. A couple of days later, a man walked into our shop and inquired about renting our space. We had not advertised it. He simply saw it and thought it would be the perfect place for his business. The good thing for him is that he didn't need to rely on local foot traffic to keep afloat. He had outside contracts that made more than enough money for him to afford the space. He even offered to buy all of our equipment. Bill named a price that we thought would be ridiculous but to our surprise, the man willingly paid what we asked for, and he took over our lease! We were able to pay the rest of our apartment lease and leave on good terms. And good news...the pastor in Austin had a three-bedroom duplex on the church property where we could live, and they offered to pay for our move. All of this came to be within about two weeks time. What a sudden, miraculous shift.

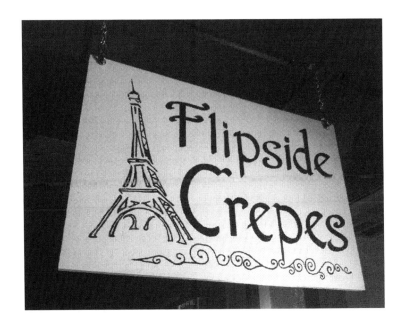

It's Not Over Yet

"So do not fear, for I am with you; do not be dismayed, for I am your God. I will strengthen you and help you; I will uphold you with my righteous right hand." Isaiah 41:10

We drove old, faithful George into Austin, excited to start a new adventure. We got settled in and started the school of ministry with Pastor Bill Hart in Austin. We switched our residency over to Texas, but quickly realized that old, rusty George would not pass Texas inspection. The cost of repairs would be far too much and the van wasn't worth the cost of repairs. Bill and I didn't have money for a vehicle, but somehow, my faith was pumped up, so I found myself saying, "I believe God will give us a car." Bill responded, "That'd be cool." My words even shocked myself. Having grown up living on poverty level, and having lived the majority of our marriage on little, it was a newfound gift for me to be able to believe for bigger things. That very weekend, during worship at church, Bill had his eyes closed and his hands out, worshipping God. Someone came over and placed keys to a car in his hand. We suddenly found ourselves driving a very nice minivan with all the bells and whistles.

There was still one major item weighing on us since closing the crepe business. We had borrowed $10,000 from a couple of friends who helped us start the business, and we wanted to pay them back. We did not mention this need to anyone, mostly due to embarrassment. We carried the burden alone. For most of my life, I didn't have the faith to believe for $100, let alone $10,000, but once again, I found myself full of faith and the words came rolling out of my mouth with confidence: "Bill, I believe God is going to give us the $10,000 to pay our friends back." He responded with, "That'd be cool."

Literally, the very next day, while Bill was headed to Mexico for a mission, my daughter and I drove to the grocery store. When we arrived home, there was a box, wrapped in red wrapping paper on our doorstep. "What in the world is this?" I wondered. Sara and I took the groceries and the box into the house. We unwrapped it, opened the box, and pulled out a stuffed Simba from The Lion King. A typewritten note stated: WELCOME BACK TO AUSTIN. WE LOVE YOU. Underneath Simba was cash. Lots of cash! Sara and I counted. $10,000! We could not believe it and I was just sure we'd made a mistake, so we recounted about four times. We were laughing and thanking God. I called Bill just before he crossed into Mexico and told him that $10,000 had arrived at our doorstep. To this day, we don't have any idea who gave us the money.

A few months later, we received a letter from the Florida Department of Revenue, stating that we owed taxes. It was a mistake. We had paid all of our taxes and we filed paperwork before leaving Florida to let them know that we were no longer in business. A quick phone call confirmed that we did not owe taxes, but they asked us to fill out paperwork once more because they had somehow failed to have the information on file. I filled out the paperwork and faxed it over. Done.

A year later, Bill and I returned home from an awesome night of worship. A notification from our bank popped up on our cell phones, simultaneously, letting us know that we were severely overdrawn in our accounts. I signed into the accounts and it showed -$8500 in checking and -$8850 in the savings account! Yes, that is a minus sign in front of those numbers. *What? How can they be negative? Someone just stole all of our money!* Bill called the bank right away. The bank representative said, "It looks like the Florida Department of Revenue took money from your account." Being that it was a Friday night, the Florida Department of Revenue would not be open until Monday, so we had about ten dollars in cash to get us through the weekend. The crazy thing about it was that Bill and I had a rush of peace come over us. We knew we didn't owe the taxes, so surely the issue would be fixed, but at the same time, we had bills due the following week, so we needed it fixed quickly. We actually chuckled and shook our heads. God had gotten us through worse. We had seen our Father at work before, so this moment didn't shake us too hard.

Monday rolled around and Bill called the Florida Department of Revenue as soon as they opened. He explained what happened, they looked up our account and said, "Oh, yes. I see here. That's a mistake. Somehow your paperwork didn't get filed." She informed us that it usually takes about six months to remedy such a mistake. The lady transferred Bill to another person who transferred him to yet another person. The last guy that he was transferred to said, "Wait…you're Bill Vanderbush? The preacher?" Bill informed him that he was. The guy was excited to talk to Bill and he proceeded to talk theology and learn more about our journey. As Bill recalls that moment, he was thinking in his head, *Sir, I just want my money back!* But the guy chatted for awhile longer and finally, he let Bill know that he would take care of everything. He then transferred Bill back to the woman so she could confirm some information. She said, "I don't know who you are, but I've never seen a situation like this get fixed so quickly." Within twenty-four hours, the money was back in our accounts.

Miracles in the Midst of Loss

"Miracles are a retelling in small letters of the very same story which is written across the whole world in letters too large for some of us to see."
C.S. Lewis

Bill's dad was coming close to the end of his life on earth. Though we did not see the breakthrough that we wanted, there were several amazing things that happened along the way. One of the many times when we rushed him to the ER during a stroke, his dad lost his ability to speak except for the following phrases: "Thank You, Jesus. Hallelujah. Praise the Lord. Amen, and Yes Lord." Doctors and nurses tried asking him questions during their evaluation, but those were the only answers Henry could give. We tried asking him questions and his answers remained the same. His speech was reduced to praise. He had a look of contentment and peace even though his body was not functioning properly. When we had entered the ER, it was packed and they were short on beds. The lobby was full and the atmosphere was chaotic. Bill's dad had suffered another mini stroke, yet he quickly improved enough for us to be discharged just over three hours later. As we were leaving, we noticed that every bed was empty. The lobby was empty. It was totally quiet. "This is so weird," I said. Bill asked one of the nurses, "Where did everyone go?" She replied, "I don't know. It's the craziest thing. It's never like this." Apparently, people got well enough to leave. Patients had been discharged and people went home! That's exactly how Henry would have wanted it.

Years later, when the moment came that Henry went to Heaven, Bill sat at his dad's bedside in a nursing home on a snowy January day. Georgian and Winnie Banov, friends who lifted us up and stood by our side during our darkest days, called Bill so they could pray and sing over his dad. Bill put the call on speaker as they prayed and sang. The room began to get hot, so much so that Bill turned off the heater. The room continued to get hot, so he opened the snow-covered window to let some cool air in. He walked into the hallway of the nursing home to see if it was hot, but it was not. *Hmm. Interesting.* Though the window was open and the heat in Henry's room had been turned off, it remained hot and Bill felt a warm, comforting presence in the room. A little while later, his dad slipped away. Bill and his mom stood by Henry and noticed that tiny flecks of gold covered his blanket. There was so much of it that when the nurses came to take his dad from the room, they kept apologizing, "We don't know where all of this glitter came from. We apologize. We don't allow glitter in here because it's a health hazard." But Bill smiled as he felt an assurance that it was just a bit of Heaven left behind as his dad departed. Heaven's "pixie dust," I like to call it.

As funeral arrangements were being made, it came to our attention that Henry had no life insurance, savings, or anything to cover the funeral. He had always lived to give, and didn't hold back anything for himself. Henry was one of the most generous people that I ever knew. Amazingly, the amount of money that was needed for funeral expenses came in quickly as various friends and family members felt compelled to contribute because Henry had been a blessing to them. Multiple stories poured in about how he had saved people's lives, encouraged them and even given to them in their time of need. We quickly learned that Henry's reach had gone further than we ever knew. He had left a beautiful, genuine impression on many lives, and because of that, there was no lack even though he had no monetary success. There was always enough. This furthered the mind shift that I was experiencing as Psalm 23 became meaningful to me.

Henry always said that Jesus never:

Worried

Hurried

Lived in the problem

Jesus lived in the solution.

I have challenged myself to live in such a way but I often fall short. Throughout the writing of this book, I have been reminded of the importance of writing down every breakthrough, every blessing great or small. When life hits you with a thousand bricks, you can look back and read over the gifts that the enemy would love for you to forget. Do yourself a favor and start writing down every good thing that has ever happened to you. This may save your life and sanity in the future, and give you the faith to walk through the valley.

Lessons in Texas

"It's a funny thing coming home. Nothing changes. Everything looks the same, feels the same, even smells the same. You realize what's changed is you."
F. Scott Fitzgerald

At the time that Bill's dad passed away, we were still serving at our friend's church in Texas. It was a wonderful season of learning for me. It seemed that even though we were repeating the school of ministry process that we had already been through multiple times over the course of a few years, everything was like new again, but with deeper revelation and meaning. It was during our time there that I became more aware that I was truly hearing God speak to me, whether through words, pictures, or nature, He was always showing me something significant. Being planted in an atmosphere where there was no pressure to perform was priceless.

The blessing of the $10,000 and the gift of a vehicle were big gifts that reawakened old dreams that I used to believe for, but financial difficulties had caused me to lay those dreams down...for a season. I have many dreams within my heart, and some of them are so huge, it will take an absolute miracle to accomplish. But I find pleasure in holding to those dreams, not in an unhealthy, ambitious way, but with a simple, child-like faith.

In Matthew 18, the disciples came to Jesus and asked, "Who then is the greatest in the kingdom of heaven?" I wish I could have heard the disciples' discussion on this topic. Perhaps they believed that whoever had attained a certain status was the greatest in the kingdom of heaven, or perhaps they figured that the most influential, powerful, or even wealthy person would be the greatest. Jesus answered their question in Matthew 18:2-4. **And He called a child to Himself and set him before them, and said, "Truly, I say to you, unless you are converted and become like children, you will not enter the kingdom of heaven. Whoever then humbles himself as this child, he is the greatest in the kingdom of heaven."** How offensive this must have been to these grown men who had left their work behind to follow Jesus. They had to have believed that by leaving their work to follow Him, there was something greater to be obtained, and there **was** something greater, but certainly not what they had envisioned.

The theme of childlikeness has been huge for me in shifting my need to be at a certain financial level. I used to be embarrassed when our lack was made known to others. It was humiliating, but life has become so much better since I lifted my eyes to a greater reality. This worldly realm is important, and we can certainly accomplish much for the Kingdom and for those around us when we use our God-given talents and abilities to create wealth. Wealth is a good thing. It is only the **love** of money that is the root of all evil. When you shift your thinking to that of a child, believing in the impossible, having total trust in your Father to sustain and provide, and dreaming big dreams that go beyond your bank accounts, that is where contentment begins.

Notice in Matthew 18 that Jesus responded to the disciples' question by first saying, "Unless you are **converted** and become like children." The word *converted* means that we need to change our mindset and think as children think. Being childlike is different than being childish. Childlikeness means living with a simplicity; the ability to believe. It means innocence. It means trust. As we grow older, we tend to question everything. Do you remember what it was like to be innocent? Do you remember what is was like to believe what you were being told? Do you remember what it was like to dream, to believe in things that we leave behind as adults?

When I was a child, growing up in Austin, Texas, I loved playing in the dirt with my toy cars. I would carve out roadways in the dirt, creating department stores, restaurants, homes, schools and libraries. I could spend hours pretending to drive through the town I created. Within the dirt, there was a story, and as I played, I always sensed a delighted presence with me. I remember feeling that God was playing with me, and I'm quite convinced that He was. We often refer to this as co-laboring with God. If you have children, you probably know what it's like to co-labor with your children's dreams. What a wonderful experience.

Our time in Texas after the Flipside season in Florida was another time of getting back to a childlike place, and God has reminded me of that over and over again.

Take a moment to pick up a journal or open your notes in your phone. Close your eyes and go back to the place of playing as a child. Take yourself back to places of innocence, belief, and trust. If you can't find it, ask the Holy Spirit to take you to a place you cannot recall.
-Write down what you see.
-Breathe deeply and give thanks to God for those moments.
-Bring those moments into now.
-Open your eyes and see through the lens of a child.
-Record the shift in how you see.

Sara's Vision Brings Healing

...So the man went and washed, and came home seeing.
John 9:7

I woke up one morning with my neck in excruciating pain. The pain radiated into my head and affected my shoulders. I visited my chiropractor who confirmed that I had slept in an odd position that moved a couple of vertebrae out of place. He adjusted me and it slightly removed some pressure, but I was hurting for three weeks and lacked full range of motion. A neck muscle kept going into spasms, causing me to lock up. I cried multiple times when the pain would peak. To put it into perspective, I went through two totally natural childbirths with absolutely zero pain medication, without crying. After three weeks of pain with my neck, I could hardly stand it anymore. People had prayed over me. Bill and I prayed. I saw the chiropractor several times and tried other suggestions as well. Finally, one night, I found myself in the sanctuary for Friday night worship: lights low, worship flowing, and all I wanted was to enter into the presence of God, undistracted by the pain.

Our daughter, Sara (who was a teenager at the time), walked into the sanctuary and sat in a chair next to me. I was sitting on the floor, wanting to stay low as to not attract attention. I was in too much pain to visit with people. I tried looking to the left and right, only to find the pain was still there, and I couldn't turn my head very far. I closed my eyes, determined to stay in a place with Jesus, away from the things of the world. After several minutes passed, I felt a hand on my neck. I opened my eyes to see who it was, and without any pain, I turned my neck to see that Sara had her hand on me. Her eyes were closed as I began turning my head from side to side, realizing that my neck had totally unlocked and their was no pain whatsoever! I gasped. She opened her eyes and asked, "Is your neck better?" I was overjoyed. "Yes, yes," I answered excitedly. "All the pain is gone, and look! I have full range of motion!"

Sara leaned toward me to tell me what had happened on her side of things. During worship, she had closed her eyes to focus on God. She saw Jesus standing in front of her smiling. He reached out His hands and invited her to go somewhere with Him. She said His hair was flowing as if they were under water, but then she realized they weren't under water. They were suspended in outer space. As He took her hand, they circled the globe and began plummeting toward earth over the Middle East. She enjoyed the excitement, but wondered why they weren't slowing down as they approached Earth. Suddenly, they dove into the ground. Everything grew dark and Sara wondered why she was in the dirt. Then she felt wet, as she was being lifted out of the ground, into the light. It was there that she realized she was the mud being put on the blind man's eyes. She heard the words, "Life must come to anything you touch." It was at that moment that she felt compelled to reach over and gently place her hand on my neck. Instantly, I was healed!

What a magnificent display of the simple, childlikeness of God Himself, playing with His children in order to show them the incredible truths and mysteries of His realm.

Childlike Dreaming With God

The Road Back to Florida

As I mentioned our crazy season of running Flipside Crepes in Florida and experiencing deep financial stress (2011-2012), I have to tell you the story about how God led us back to the scene for a new chapter. During those stressful days of trying to keep our small business alive, a friend felt bad for our family because we were all working ourselves nearly to death. She bought our family annual passes to Disney World since we lived and worked right down the road from the land where dreams come true. "I'm worried about you all. You guys need to take breaks and enjoy some fun with your kids," she told us.

It became a weekly thing for us to find a night when we could leave our little restaurant just in time for fireworks at the Magic Kingdom. We would close up shop, jump in the car with our dirty dishrags and towels, and head straight to Disney World. We would enter the gates just minutes before the fireworks show began. Songs of faith, hope, trust, belief, and coming through the trials of life filled us with hope. Bill, Britain, Sara, and I would stand side-by-side, arm-in-arm, and weep as fireworks mixed with story, infusing our hearts with hope.

During those hard, hopeless days when we struggled to get by, Bill and I would drive into a little town called Celebration to do our banking. Celebration is a town that was built by Disney, born out of a vision that Walt Disney had long before he died. As we drove into Celebration several times a week for business banking, we looked at the white, picket fences, the finely trimmed lawns and perfectly landscaped sidewalks. Front porches appeared welcoming, like *come on over and have some cookies and lemonade* inviting. "Who in the world lives in this place?" we would ask each other. "How do people live here? What is it like to live in such a place?"

We turned a corner, admiring the townhomes being embraced by Crape Myrtle trees and Gardenia bushes. "I could live there," I commented. Bill pointed at the church across the street and said, "And I could pastor there." We giggled. "That would be nuts, right? Can you imagine that?" We laughed and continued on to the bank. We deposited our measly bit from the day, hoping we could give our apartment manager enough to keep us from getting evicted. We walked down the main street, admiring the architecture and uniqueness of the town where some really lucky people lived.

We got into our van (Old George) as rain started pouring. As Bill turned the key, the starter whirred, but the van would not start. It turned out that our alternator was out, we had no way home, and our children were at home. I honestly can't remember how we got home that day, but we spent the profit of that day on a tow truck and new alternator. I will never forget watching my hard-working husband sitting in the driver's seat of the van, shaking his head in defeat. "You have got to be kidding." The next morning, he walked five miles to the mechanic, charged the fees and drove to the market to buy ingredients for our business. What irony to drive through an idealistic, dreamy town only to end up being reminded of your lack and brokenness. Right? But...

Fast Forward Four Years

"God uses rescued people to rescue people."
Christine Caine

After we were rescued out of that season and enjoyed a delightful time of serving and learning in Texas, we felt a shift coming. Our son had been working at Disney for a couple of years and our daughter got a job there, too, leaving us in an empty nest. We were content, though we missed them terribly. We were happy for our kids in their adventure. We prayed for them daily, and I would often find myself praying for the Disney company as well. I began having dreams of Walt Disney in which I saw him sitting underneath of a tree, writing in a journal. I got the feeling that God was showing him big things and giving him a vision to create something. I prayed about the dreams and told Bill what I was feeling: "I think we are supposed to be part of something that God put in Walt Disney's heart, and it never fully manifest, but I think we're supposed to pick that up. I have no idea what that is, though."

Bill and I began praying about moving to the Orlando area since both of our kids were there, and we wanted to have that last bit of time with them together before they ventured off to other places. At this time, Bill was working on co-authoring a book with New

York Times Best-selling Author, Ted Dekker. They had become friends through a series of events (one being a prophetic dream that my son had), and they quickly connected over their love for Jesus and His ways. The book, The Forgotten Way, was important to them. Ted offered Bill a one year contract to focus solely on the project, which Bill agreed to. This gave him the ability to work from anywhere, so Bill said to me, "If we're going to move to Orlando, let's look at Celebration. I think we should go there." The thought excited me. *Wow! Seriously? The town we used to drive through and dream about?*

That night, we looked online at apartments and condos for rent in Celebration. At this point, it still didn't seem real. *We were just pretending, right?* I was concerned about moving because our credit was still poor from the damage we did during our time in business…and even before that, actually. I couldn't imagine how anyone would agree to rent to us after running a credit check. But we believed anyway. That night, Bill had a dream about a man named Neil Rhodes. Neil had been a friend of Bill's dad, and had helped his dad roof their house when Bill was only ten years old. The last time Bill ever saw Neil, Bill was fourteen years old. In two decades of marriage, I had never heard Bill talk about Neil, so this dream was extremely unusual and random!

In the dream, Bill was handing shingles to Neil, atop of a house. Bill woke up from the dream thinking it odd that he would dream about he and Neil roofing a house. He picked up his phone to check the time. *4:44am.* He opened Facebook and began searching for Neil. He found him, sent him a friend request and message. The next morning, Neil replied and gave Bill his phone number. Within a couple of hours, Bill was on the phone with Neil, catching up on the last three decades of life. Neil had served as a pastor at Times Square Church for awhile in New York City, which Bill was intrigued by. I heard Bill ask, "So where do you live now?" Neil answered, "Well, my wife and I just moved to a little town in Florida, called Celebration." Bill just about flew off the couch!

"What? Traci and I were just looking at apartments in Celebration last night!"

Long story short, one incredible open door after another opened for us, and within a couple of months, we were making the move to Celebration. When we had met with the owner of a small, two-bedroom condo in the town's center, the owner asked, "Would you like to rent it?" Amazingly, it was in our price range, but we feared the credit report. We informed him that we had messed up our credit with a business venture. The owner said, "Oh, that's fine. That happens to lots of people." He gave us a lease to sign and never ran a credit report!

Let me back up to say that several months prior, a man from another town, whom I did not know, came to me and said, "I see a transition coming for you soon. It's going to be great but there will be a lot of turbulence before you 'land.' Don't be afraid. You will get there safely and all will be well." As we were packing to move, we got the shocking news that my dad would need a quintuple heart bypass. The news shook me. My dad is a hard-working man who had already suffered a devastating chronic pain disorder caused by a car accident. How could this even be possible? He was already facing enough! My dad's heart surgery was scheduled for June 3rd, and our move was to take place on June 10th. I was frightened for my dad, and I wept like a baby because I hated that he had to go through that. I feared the "what ifs" and I lost my childlike faith. My prayers became challenges and threats to God. *If you let anything happen to my dad* kind of prayers. I totally forgot about the man's word about turbulence. How I wish I would have held onto those words and just trusted the Father.

I ended up staying with my dad for five weeks to help him recover. It was a wonderful time, and I was so happy for every moment that I witnessed him becoming stronger. While I was with him, Bill and Sara loaded up our moving truck, along with our dog, Sasha, and moved to Florida. The morning they arrived in Orlando was the morning that a gunman massacred 49 people and wounded 53 others at the Pulse night club. It was a horribly sad time in the city, and it prompted us to pray more about our reason for being there.

At the end of the five weeks with my dad, I flew home to our apartment in Celebration for the first time. Shortly after my arrival, Bill and I walked to the local Starbucks where we overheard a guy talking to a group of people at his table. He mentioned things about the "Kingdom of God" and a "move of God," so we decided to introduce ourselves. It turned out, it was Pastor William Lewis from Community Presbyterian Church in the center of Celebration. Bill and I knew nothing about Presbyterian church, and we honestly were not seeking a church to attend at the time. We had decided to take time for home church, but apparently there was a bigger plan in store. Bill and Pastor William were passionate about seeing a move of the Holy Spirit, so they met often to talk about what was on their hearts. After a few months, Bill was offered a position at the church, to which he declined. Another offer. Then another. By the fourth offer, it became very clear that we were being led that direction.

In fact, in the midst of those job offers, we finished out our lease on our apartment. We were searching for something with an extra bedroom so we could have guests stay with us. A dear realtor friend took us to see a property on the main canal street that goes into town. The property address was 444 which reminded me about Bill waking from the dream (that led us to Celebration) at 4:44am. *Hm. I wonder.* But it turned out that it was not the property for us, however, as we walked out of the property, I saw Pastor William and his wife coming from the right, walking their dog. And from the left, Neil Rhodes and his wife came along walking their dog. We all converged in front of 444. There we all stood together, and it dawned on me that this was a divine convergence. Neil ended up being an honorary pastor at the church until he answered a called to move to Geneva. Seeing *444* and running into Neil and William at that moment was confirmation that we were definitely being led to Celebration for something greater than we had imagined. Though that particular property was not the one we felt led to live in, one of our elders connected us with a lady who was in the process of renovating a beautiful townhome that she would be renting out. Ironically, it's the very place that I had pointed at years earlier, saying, "I could live there." We went to see the townhome as it was in process, completely stripped down: bare sheetrock, no countertops and no appliances. The owner asked if we would like to rent it, and she gave us a fantastic deal. We moved in before it was finished. One month later, we were in awe of what a beautiful job she had done.

Shortly after Bill accepted the offer to work for Community Presbyterian of Celebration, I happened to mention to one of the elders of the church that I had dreams about Walt Disney and his vision. She smiled widely and said, "Well, you know this is like the Disney church, right?" What I did not know was that the church had been dedicated to Walt and Roy Disney by their two nieces who were at the groundbreaking. The Disney family actually contributed to the building of the church (you can find the plaque on the side of the building at 511 Celebration Avenue). What I also did not know was that Walt carried a deep faith in God and he had written about his study of the Scriptures. He attributed what he accomplished to prayer. Later, I found that a church was included in his drawings for a community. What you can see, even in his sketches of the Main Street of Magic Kingdom, is that a church was included. At the time of this writing, there is a picture of that drawing in Disney's Hollywood Studios, and there is also a model of the community he dreamed of, that can be seen from the People Mover ride in Magic Kingdom (I hope those items will remain there). Multiple steeples are included in the model. Obviously, faith played a large role in Walt's life. My mind was blown by how my dreams intertwined with God bringing us into this town.

Since coming here, I have discovered the power of true visionaries. True visionaries do not see obstacles and limitations. They only see opportunities. There are no impossibilities. I have met people in this town who came from very little. Some still have little (on paper), yet because God likes to do the impossible, they are living in places and in ways that don't line up on paper. The numbers don't add up. That is how God works. This was evident in Walt Disney's life. He was a man who came from poverty. He knew loss. He knew bankruptcy. He knew what it was like to have a nervous breakdown over losing everything; his dream was taken from him at one time. But Walt never gave up. He believed the impossible and he didn't let the naysayers talk him out of his vision.

Just Believe

The tongue has the power of life and death...
Proverbs 18:21

Our lives drastically shifted over the last several years as I began to believe God for anything, even when bank accounts, bills, and other things would scream, "Impossible!" With God, ALL things are possible. With God, NOTHING is impossible. Jesus said it, so either He was telling the truth, or He was a liar. Which do you believe? I believe what He said. Does ALL mean ALL? All things are possible. Living in this childlike trust, believing Him at His word, has given me the opportunity to see thousands of things happen that would not have happened had I stayed in the mindset of lack. We have to believe it before we see it.

We still may not have the entirety of the American Dream. We had no college fund for our kids. We lack in some areas, but honestly, lack is an illusion. God made everything possible. It's at our fingertips. It's within us. Christ in you, the hope of glory (Colossians 1:27). When Jesus was asked by the Pharisees when the kingdom of God would come, He answered, "The kingdom of God does not come with observation, nor will they say, 'See here!' or 'See there!' For indeed, **the kingdom of God is within you**." Do we believe the words of Jesus or not? If the kingdom is within us, we have access to all, and you are not limited by dollars or lack of dollars. I am not talking about doing foolish things like writing hot checks and making stupid decisions in the name of Christ. I am talking about believing and watching God make a way where there is no way.

When it looked like there was no way for Lazarus to come back from the dead, Jesus first wept sorrowfully with his friends, but then he raised Lazarus. After raising him, Jesus said, "Did I not tell you that if you believe, you will see the glory of God?" (John 11:40) I would like to encourage you that no matter how far gone a situation may seem, no matter how **dead** your finances are, and no matter what obstacles have been placed before you, close your eyes and return to a moment in childhood where you had unlimited belief. If you cannot find that place of innocence and belief, ask God to restore it to your memory. May that gift of faith rise up within you, and may joy fill your heart as you see the obstacles as being tiny little bubbles under the weight of a magnificent Father who loves you and backs you up.

> You can do all things through Christ who strengthens you.
> Philippians 4:13

Go and live in peace.
You are not defined by your finances.
Your finances are not your identity.
Your finances are not who you are.
Lack does not dictate your life.
You have access to everything.
Nothing is impossible.
Just believe.

Changing Your Mind

Where do I start?

The way we view finances and learning who we are in Christ is the beginning of opening yourself up to limitless possibilities. Once again, I would like to highly recommend Jim Baker's book, When Heaven Invades Your Finances (BakersEquip.com) and I also recommend saturating yourself in my husband, Bill's, Project 24 teachings. Project 24 is twenty-four hours of Bible-based teaching on your identity in Christ. Knowing who you are in Christ, and the powerful union that you have with God the Father, is vital to everything we do in life. These teachings have brought incredible freedom to many people on multiple levels: body, soul, spirit, and mind…healing in relationships, finances, and other areas of life.

When Heaven Invades Your Finances: BakersEquip.com

Project 24: billvanderbush.com

Helpful Scriptures

Either we accept His words or we call Him a liar.

Jesus looked at them and said, 'With men it is impossible, but not with God; for with God, all things are possible.' Mark 10:27

And my God will meet all your needs according to His glorious riches in Christ Jesus. Philippians 4:19

For truly I say to you, if you have faith like a grain of mustard seed, you will say to this mountain, Move from here to there, and it will move, and nothing will be impossible for you. Matthew 17:20

Therefore I tell you, whatever you ask in prayer, believe that you have received it, and it will be yours. Mark 11:24

Little children, you are from God and have overcome them, for he who is in you is greater than he who is in the world. 1 John 4:4

For NOTHING will be impossible with God. Luke 1:37

Is anything too hard for the Lord? Genesis 18:14

Now to him who is able to do far more abundantly than all that we ask or think, according to the power at work within us…
Ephesians 3:20

All things are possible for one who believes. Mark 9:23

But seek first the Kingdom of God and his righteousness, and all these things will be added to you. Matthew 6:33

Let not your hearts be troubled. Believe in God and believe also in Me. John 14:1

What is impossible with men is possible with God. Luke 18:27

Behold, I am the Lord, the God of all flesh. Is anything too hard for me? Jeremiah 32:27

And Jesus answered them, "Truly, I say to you, if you have faith and do not doubt, you will not only do what has been done to the fig tree, but even if you say to this mountain, 'Be taken up and thrown into the sea,' it will happen. And whatever you ask in prayer, you will receive, if you have faith." Matthew 21:21-22

In all your ways, acknowledge him, and he will make straight your paths. Proverbs 3:6

"It's kind of fun to do the impossible."

~WALT DISNEY

I hope this little book has been an encouragement for you. Other books and resources are available on amazon.com and tracivanderbush.wix.com/vanderbush

Novels:
The Porches of Holly (in early pre-production for a movie)
The Windows of Holly

Other books:
Vignette: Glimpses of Mysterious Love
Walking With A Shepherd
The Magic of our Forefathers
Soul Reformation: Wholeness for the Body

Children's books:
Mr. Thomas and the Cottonwood Tree
Life with Lummox
Lummox and the Happy Christmas

Also visit billvanderbush.com for Reckless Grace and multiple sermon downloads.

About the Author

Traci Vanderbush enjoys the simplicity of being married to her best friend and childhood sweetheart, Bill Vanderbush, and being mom to two amazing people. She has a passion for writing, dancing, and exploring creation as she releases the words of the Creator through writing to infuse hope and ignite dreams in the hearts of others.

Made in the
USA
Lexington, KY